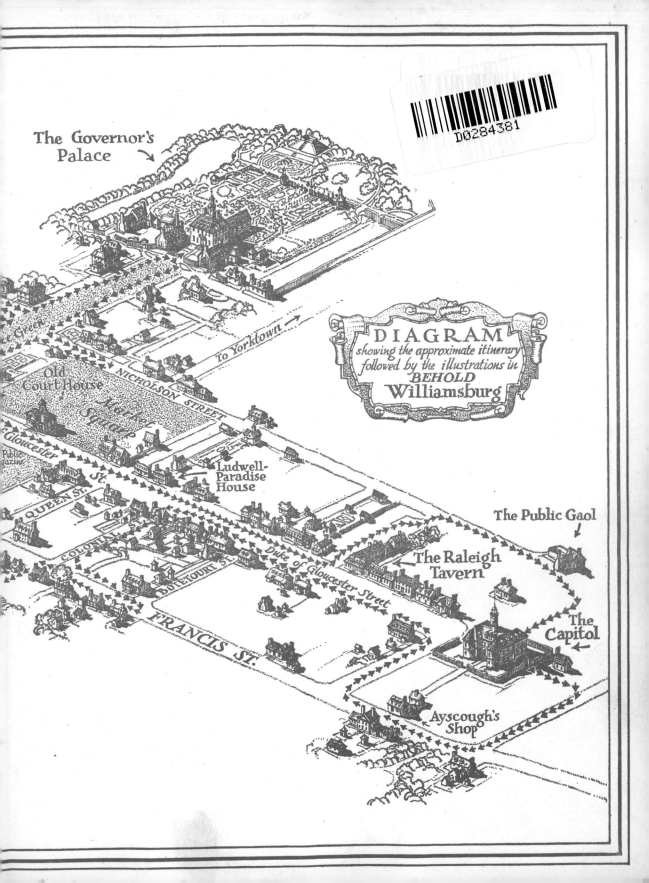

The Governor's Palace

To Yorktown →

DIAGRAM
showing the approximate itinerary
followed by the illustrations in
BEHOLD
Williamsburg

Palace Green

Old Court House

Market Square

NICHOLSON STREET

Gloucester St.

Public Magazine

Queen St.

COLONIAL ST.

BOTETOURT ST.

Ludwell-Paradise House

Duke of Gloucester Street

FRANCIS ST.

The Public Gaol

The Raleigh Tavern

The Capitol

Ayscough's Shop

BEHOLD
WILLIAMSBURG

THE OLD COURT HOUSE

BEHOLD WILLIAMSBURG

A Pictorial Tour of Virginia's Colonial Capital

Illustrations and Text by

SAMUEL CHAMBERLAIN

Published in Coöperation with Colonial Williamsburg

HASTINGS HOUSE, *Publishers*   NEW YORK 18

Kitchen of the John Blair House

Along the Palace Green

Foreword

Something unique and extraordinary has occurred in Tidewater Virginia during the past twenty years. The 18th Century Capital of Virginia Colony, a small but immensely significant city, has risen again on its original foundations. It has been freed of the architectural encroachments of later centuries, and stands today a living manifestation of the early American way of life. Restored Williamsburg is an American phenomenon of immediate value and significance.

The idea of restoring an entire 18th Century community of this importance was quite without precedent. It was a bold conception, requiring imagination and capital and a certain undaunted vigor to overcome numberless obstacles and difficulties. It could not have succeeded without the ready cooperation of the overwhelming majority of Williamsburg citizens. It required the professional skill, imagination and good taste of eminently qualified architects, landscape architects and decorators. It could not have attained authenticity without the patient ground work of a research staff as astute as it was thorough.

But the idea *did* succeed, and credit for making this courageous dream a reality belongs principally to two men of vision, the late Dr. W. A. R. Goodwin and Mr. John D. Rockefeller, Jr. It was Dr. Goodwin, formerly Rector of Bruton Parish Church, who con-

ceived the idea of the restored community and it was Mr. Rockefeller who shared his enthusiasm and provided the funds and the organization to carry on the work. The influence of Williamsburg is one which extends indefinitely into the future. Your grandchildren will make pilgrimages here to study and enjoy an American institution of permanent interest. This is where the imagination of Dr. Goodwin, and the foresight and generosity of Mr. Rockefeller, take on an added significance. For Williamsburg has a graphic message to impart. Its influence on American education, on our architecture and decoration, is increasingly apparent. Above all, it dramatizes in a moving and inescapable manner, just what it means to be an American. These are influences which will not diminish in the future, because restored Williamsburg is true and authentic. The thing to remember, as one walks down the Duke of Gloucester Street, is that all this has been *recreated,* not surmised. Future generations will accept it as fact, and they will not have been deceived.

The work of rebuilding this Colonial community was, of course, interrupted by the war, and it is not yet complete. More than fifty structures, with their secondary outbuildings, remain to be translated from architects' drawings to restored reality. This book, therefore, interprets Williamsburg at a moment of

1

temporary halt, but in a period of its development familiar to literally millions of visitors. Future editions will contain supplementary views of changes in the Williamsburg scene.

Many books and publications have been devoted to Williamsburg. Some have dealt with its history and restoration, others with its architecture and decoration. A new book on Williamsburg should have something new to offer. By providing a pictorial tour of Virginia's Colonial Capital, this volume presents a different and more detailed approach to the pleasant business of exploring Williamsburg, either in absentia, anticipation, reality, or in retrospect.

If the reader so wishes he can utilize this volume as an informal guide, a talkative but discreet companion at his elbow. The illustrations have been arranged to follow a definite path. A diagram of this pictorial "conducted tour" will be found outlined on the front end paper. A brief index appears on the rear end paper. The leisurely promenade begins at the College of William and Mary and continues eastward down one side of the Duke of Gloucester Street as far as the historic Capitol and then back on the opposite side, indulging in several profitable detours on the way. The inquisitive camera takes the reader down unsuspected side streets and peers over a few back fences, in addition to viewing Williamsburg from conventional angles. In an attempt to illustrate the minor phases of the restored city as well as its more imposing structures, one view or more of almost every restored house, large or small, has been included. This is perhaps the most extensive pictorial coverage of Williamsburg yet to be published.

These photographs, drypoints and sketches were chosen from a collection which has been more than ten years in the making. The exterior photographs have all been taken in clear sunlight, some of them before the first March bud, some in the dense fullness of summer foliage and others as late as the last brown November leaf. They are made by an inveterate Williamsburg visitor and they are the type of picture that any traveler might take, given the right combination of sunlight, clouds and foliage. Visitors, however, do not always have the time to wait for that precise burst of sunlight, nor the good fortune to be a perennial frequenter. It is the author's fond hope that some Williamsburg voyagers will consider this collection of pictures the one they themselves would have taken if time and circumstances had permitted. The photographer's sworn enemies—telephone poles, wires and signboards—have been banished from the scene, but it takes time and patience for him to outwit the parked automobile.

Almost all of these photographs are informal, and in no sense official. The author has been fortunate, however, in receiving the assistance of Colonial Williamsburg in the preparation of this book. Its research staff has supplied abundant data for the captions, and has subsequently verified them. In addition, the Department of Public Relations has furnished all the interior photographs of Colonial Williamsburg's buildings which appear in these pages. These interiors are the work of the well known New York photographer, Richard Garrison. To Colonial Williamsburg, and to its able and very considerate officials, this writer would like to express warm appreciation.

SAMUEL CHAMBERLAIN

Colonial Street

The Wren Building

Williamsburg has grown up in front of the WREN BUILDING, and there is no better place to begin this leisurely tour than in the sheltered grounds of the College of William and Mary, the second oldest institution of higher learning in America. Here in a calm setting of majestic elms rises the WREN BUILDING, dominating the triangular yard and facing the western extremity of Williamsburg's noted thoroughfare, the Duke of Gloucester Street. Contemporary statements have been found which lead to the belief that this building was designed by the great English architect, Sir Christopher Wren. Moreover it is the oldest academic building standing in this country, its foundation having been laid in 1695, in what was then known as "Middle Plantation." Four years later the Capital was moved here from Jamestown, and the Assembly convened in the Great Hall of this building until the new capitol was built at the opposite end of the newly laid-out town of Williamsburg.

Only a few years elapsed before the WREN BUILDING was damaged by fire, in 1705. It suffered similar misfortunes in 1859 and 1862. Twice it was used as a war-time hospital, first by the French forces in 1781 and again by Confederate soldiers during the War Between the States.

This was among the first buildings to be reconditioned when the restoration of Williamsburg was begun in 1928. In this task the architects were aided by the providential discovery of a copper plate at the Bodleian Library at Oxford, England, which showed accurate elevations of this and other Williamsburg landmarks as they appeared early in the 18th Century.

Luxuriant foliage in the College yard partially obscures the delicate dormers and the long rectangular silhouette of the WREN BUILDING. This pencil drawing was made in springtime, against a soft afternoon light.

The sunny, vine-grown facade of the WREN BUILDING now shows scant sign of the three disastrous fires which have ravaged the venerable structure, but a closer study of the patched brickwork will reveal eloquent traces.

Upon a baroque pedestal in the College yard stands the time-stained marble figure of Virginia's beloved Royal Governor, NORBORNE BERKELEY, BARON DE BOTETOURT, whose body is entombed in the College Chapel. The Assembly commissioned Richard Hayward, London sculptor, to carve this graceful monument to one of the most respected of Virginia's Governors. It was completed in 1773 and originally stood in the open corridor of the Capitol. During the Revolution it was overturned by too-zealous patriots, but it survived this indignity with only a few blemishes.

The WREN BUILDING possesses the sturdy solidity and sensitive proportions typical of the best 18th Century American architecture. Although it was "first modelled by Sir Christopher Wren," the building was "adapted to the Nature of the Country by the Gentlemen there." Prominent among the latter was Governor Spotswood, a man of good taste and enthusiasm. To him belongs much of the credit for preserving the Wren tradition after the fire of 1705.

(Left) The rebuilt KITCHEN of the BRAFFERTON BUILDING, an unassuming brick structure facing the College yard, now serves as an Alumni office for the College of William and Mary.

The two wings which project from the west side of the WREN BUILDING contain the Great Hall and the Chapel An enclosed quadrangle was the goal set by the original design, but this was never achieved.

The early brickwork which survived the WREN BUILDING fire of 1705 can be identified in the varied wall texture of the Great Hall. This was originally set in Flemish and English bond.

The BRAFFERTON BUILDING was built in 1723, with funds left by Robert Boyle, the English scientist, for the purpose of establishing a permanent Indian school, the first in the Colonies. It is the only one of the three original college buildings to escape damage by fire, but at some time it was stripped of its interior woodwork. Restored in 1932, it now serves as the Faculty Club and contains quarters for distinguished visitors to the College. From the outside it is almost identical with the President's House which faces it across the College yard.

The PRESIDENT'S HOUSE—This dignified brick mansion with steep hip roof and double chimneys has always been the home of the Presidents of the College of William and Mary. It was erected in 1732 by Williamsburg's master-builder, Henry Cary, Jr. James Blair, the fiery first President of the College, was its earliest tenant, living here for ten years. During the Revolution it served as Headquarters for Lord Cornwallis just before the Battle of Green Spring. Later, during the Siege of Yorktown, it was occupied by the French Surgeon General. At that time it was damaged by fire, but was later repaired at the expense of Louis XVI.

The central hallway of the WREN BUILDING looks out on the sunny College yard.

(Left) This oval tablet, placed in the sheltered arcade of the WREN BUILDING, outlines the glorious history of the College and mentions some of its illustrious sons. Three Presidents of the United States, Thomas Jefferson, James Monroe and John Tyler, were alumni of William and Mary, as was John Marshall, first Chief Justice of the United States. George Washington received his Surveyor's Commission here in 1749, and later served as Chancellor. Benjamin Franklin traveled here to receive the Honorary Degree of Master of Arts in 1756. Through the centuries the College has always been progressive. It was the first to establish an honor system and an elective plan of studies. It pioneered in schools of law, medicine, modern languages and history. Phi Beta Kappa was founded here in 1776. The College was forced to close its doors twice in the nineteenth century. But its spirit has never dimmed, and today it stands stronger than ever before. The College of William and Mary is now co-educational. It contributes an invigorating atmosphere of healthy, intelligent youth to the historic town.

The South Chapel wing was added to the WREN BUILDING in 1732. Weekly services of the College are held in this high-panelled Chapel, now restored to its original late Jacobean style. Beneath its chancel floor are buried many notables, among them Sir John Randolph and his two sons, one a Tory and one a Patriot. Many a college wedding takes place before this dignified altar.

(Right) The imposing Great Hall, which occupies the north wing of the WREN BUILDING, is panelled in native pine. Here the General Assembly met in the early days before the first Williamsburg Capitol was built.

The modern business area has been built to round out the picture of a restored community. Well designed shops, built in the 18th Century tradition, blend into a peaceful architectural group along the brick walk.

The architectural personality of banks, drug stores, restaurants and chain shops has been somewhat submerged to achieve a harmonious grouping. The local bank takes on a pronounced personality in the process.

In Colonial days the business area, well studded with Or-dinaries and Taverns, grew up in the neighborhood of the Capitol. Now the pendulum has swung the other way, and the historic, festive tavern has been largely replaced by the college soda fountain. The community which fills the first block of the Duke of Gloucester Street is well patronized by townspeople and visitors, but there are times when it seems to be the exclusive domain of the college students. In spite of its casual appearance, the area has been planned with great skill and forethought by the architects, Perry, Shaw and Hepburn, of Boston. The parking problem has been met by large, unobstrusive free parking lots at the rear of the shops. There are no glaring signs to detract from the scene, no exposed telephone poles or wires. Such things as mail boxes and hydrants are all but invisible. While Williamsburg has the comforts and commercial ad-vantages common to much larger cities, it has the good taste to be unostentatious about it.

At this point our path leads eastward on the Duke of Gloucester Street to the JOHN BLAIR HOUSE, a cheerful and distinguished pitch-roofed structure with double front steps. In the days preceding the Revolution it was occupied by John Blair, Jr., signer of the Constitution and Justice of the United States Supreme Court. French officers were frequent guests of the Blair family in this house in 1781. The exact date of the building of the house is uncertain, but 1745 seems to be a probability. Its solid simplicity is perhaps its greatest charm.

KITCHEN OF THE JOHN BLAIR HOUSE—The separate kitchen in the garden, with its immense brick chimney, open hearth and attic living quarters, is an outmoded institution of Colonial life.

The BLAIR HOUSE KITCHEN is surrounded by whitewashed utility buildings and a most intriguing herb garden in the old Williamsburg tradition. Many such restored kitchens now serve as private living quarters.

Next along our path is BRUTON PARISH CHURCH, a weathered veteran in multicolored brick which is practically the keystone of the Williamsburg Renaissance. This drypoint was made in 1937, before the steeple was restored.

16

Bruton Parish Church

The mellow brick structure which stands serenely among these trees has probably been in continuous use longer than any Episcopal church in America. It is built near the site of an earlier Bruton Church which, being intended only for a small rural congregation at Middle Plantation, proved inadequate for a Colonial capital. Work was begun on the present building in 1711 and it was completed five years later. Since then it has served continuously as a House of Worship. Virginia's versatile Governor Alexander Spotswood prepared the plans and supervised the construction, which is in the pure tradition of Early Virginia design. It was acknowledged the "Court Church" of Colonial Virginia and most of the great Virginians of Colonial times have worshipped here. Washington's name appears on the Church record as having had eleven slaves baptized here between the years 1762 and 1768.

It is due to the vision and tenacity of the late rector of this church, Dr. W. A. R. Goodwin, that the idea of restoring Colonial Williamsburg was developed. It was Dr. Goodwin who first conceived the plan of a revived Colonial community and who persuaded Mr. John D. Rockefeller, Jr. to embark on this notable project.

Dr. Goodwin's zeal as an archaeologist and historian had led to a partial restoration of this church and the brick residence of George Wythe, which became the Parish House. His enthusiasm, undaunted by the many obstacles to the far larger plan of recreating the Colonial city, was readily transmitted to the organization established by Mr. Rockefeller to carry on the restoration. Dr. Goodwin lived to see his cherished dream fulfilled. His death occured in 1939, and his remains are buried within the church

The steeple was a later addition to BRUTON PARISH CHURCH, having been built in 1769. Two-storied and octagonal, it was restored in 1938-40. Here hangs Virginia's "Liberty Bell," so called because it rang out announcing the Declaration of Independence. It was presented to the Parish in 1761 by James Tarpley.

From almost any angle BRUTON PARISH CHURCH presents a stimulating silhouette to the eye. The iridescent brownish pink of its brickwork provides a ceaseless pageant of subtle color, shifting with the shadows.

(Right) The Church borders the southern extremity of the Palace Green.

No one who has seen the soft luminous interior of BRUTON PARISH CHURCH will soon forget it. The stamp of age and complete authenticity is here, despite new coats of paint. It was not always thus. The interior was modified, and not for the better, in 1838-40. Under the impetus of the energetic Dr. Goodwin it was partially restored in 1905, and later brought to its present finished state with the aid of Colonial Williamsburg. Its 18th Century pipe organ is now in place. The roomy, throne-like box pew of the Colonial Governor, which once bore the Royal insignia and was sheltered by a rich velvet canopy, still stands, facing the pulpit. The pews, painted a soft oyster white with copings of dark wood, are lettered as memorials to famous Virginians and men of state who worshipped here, among them Washington, Jefferson, Monroe and Marshall. The chancel floors are of English stone. In the tower entrance is a 17th Century baptismal font of marble, brought here from Jamestown.

(Left) Springtime vista of the Church steeple seen from the garden of a neighboring house.

The walls of BRUTON PARISH CHURCH form a background to the CUSTIS TENEMENT GARDENS, located on the opposite side of the Duke of Gloucester Street. The gnarled trunk of an old mulberry tree fills the foreground.

Before the most recent restoration of BRUTON PARISH CHURCH in 1938-40 its colorful brick walls were bearded with vines and its arched windows were flanked with white shutters. Its trim is now painted a cream color.

An early morning view of the north side of BRUTON PARISH CHURCH demonstrates the unobtrusive manner in which essential chimneys, gutters and screens have been added to the original structure.

Many distinguished Virginians are buried in this sheltered churchyard, whose sculptured tombs are very English in character. Beyond the churchyard wall is the George Wythe House.

The George Wythe House

Tradition has it that this impressive house was built ca. 1755 by Richard Taliaferro, who, in addition to being a planter, numbered architecture among his accomplishments as a country gentleman. In 1779 he bequeathed the house to his daughter Elizabeth and her husband, George Wythe, who were then its occupants. Wythe was a lawyer, educator, patriot, and one of the most eminent Virginians of his epoch. He served at one time or another as a member of the House of Burgesses, Attorney General, Clerk of the House, Mayor of Williamsburg, and Speaker of the House of Delegates. He had the distinction of being the first Virginia Signer of the Declaration of Independence and the first college professor of law in the Colonies. As such he be-

came the teacher of John Marshall, when the latter studied law at the College of William and Mary. To Thomas Jefferson he was not only a teacher but a life-long friend and confidant. George Wythe died in 1806, reputedly from poison administered by a great-nephew who was over eager to inherit the bulk of his estate.

The house has changed but little during the intervening years. It was partially restored by Dr. W. A. R. Goodwin in the late 1920's to serve as a Parish House. After filling this purpose for some years the house was transferred by the Church to Colonial Williamsburg in 1938. Restored and refurnished as a typical 18th Century town residence of a Colonial gentlemen of means, it was opened to the public in 1940.

The solid rectangular form of the GEORGE WYTHE HOUSE rises up prominently beyond the low churchyard wall. The small frame structure on the right has been restored and now contains exhibits of the weaver's art.

GEORGE WYTHE HOUSE—In this dignified residence facing the Palace Green, General Washington established his Headquarters prior to the Siege of Yorktown. It was later used for the same purpose by the Comte de Rochambeau.

From a vantage point on the west steps of the GEORGE WYTHE HOUSE, the visitor looks out upon a lively pattern of boxwood hedges and bushes, red brick tile walks, white fences and outbuildings.

Household problems of the 18th Century are graphically presented at the GEORGE WYTHE HOUSE. The laundry, smokehouse and kitchen have been rebuilt on their old foundations under the shelter of a massive sycamore.

GEORGE WYTHE'S STUDY—Simple whitewashed walls provide an effective background for the 18th Century furniture and fabrics, and the beautiful needlework rug chosen for this room. In the corner by the stone mantel is a gaming table with combination checker and chess board. The wing chair, covered with an exquisite blue damask, together with the blue curtains and the grey-blue tone of the woodwork, establish the color note of the room.

THE SOUTHEAST BEDROOM OF THE GEORGE WYTHE
HOUSE—The woodwork in this room is painted a
subtle grey-green, and the floor consists of plain pine
boards, well waxed. The fire screen, embellished with
a needlework panel, proved its worth on cold winter
nights.

(Left) A glimpse of the dining room.

The formal dining room of the GEORGE WYTHE HOUSE is impressive in its restraint and unforgettable for its soft yellow hangings and grey green woodwork. The three-part cherry inlaid table and the Tidewater Virginia mahogany chairs both are from the late 18th Century. Against the wall is a rare walnut cellaret.

All of the charm and little of the inconvenience of Colonial life is recalled by the cheerful, white walled Southwest bedroom of the GEORGE WYTHE HOUSE. The late 18th Century bed rests on a hand-woven rag rug. The curtains are copied from Thomas Jefferson's design. On the wall is an old English needlework picture.

The part played by music in the life of a Colonial gentleman is suggested by this view of the Parlor of the GEORGE WYTHE HOUSE. Here the curtains are of green damask. Since no detailed inventory of the furnishings of this house has come to light, it has been furnished with antique pieces which might logically be found in the 18th Century residence of a man of wealth and position.

There is a magic week in Springtime when the silhouette of Bruton Parish Church, etched through the budding foliage, is particularly lovely from the garden terrace of the GEORGE WYTHE HOUSE.

A long stretch of clipped green lawn, bordered with flower beds and boxwood, extends westward through the gardens of the GEORGE WYTHE HOUSE. This may well have served as a bowling green in Colonial days.

A chicken house, dovecote and stable form a picturesque farm group in one corner of the GEORGE WYTHE estate, which has reverted to the self-sufficient status of the 18th Century. Note the variety of fences.

At present the front entrance to the George Wythe House is almost severely correct, in contrast to the more luxurious effect which prevailed before the most recent restoration. At that time a rich Colonial doorway with a split pediment, partially draped with ivy, dominated the facade. This doorway bore a close resemblance to the portal of Westover, the celebrated James River estate. Correctness has been achieved in this case at the expense of a certain architectural warmth imparted by the departed doorway. But the restorers of Williamsburg are too conscientious to let such an anachronism, however pleasant, remain to strike a false note.

(Right) Doorway of the George Wythe House in 1936.

Leaving behind the outbuildings on the George Wythe estate, the visitor has only to cross Prince George Street to find the old fashioned boxwood gardens of the DEANE HOUSE. In summer it is gay with 18th Century flowers.

GARDEN OF THE DEANE HOUSE—A geometrical Virginia garden, even in the formative days when it is sheltered by saplings rather than by massive monarchs, is always a heart-warming sight.

The DEANE HOUSE, a recently reconstructed frame dwelling, is just north of the George Wythe House, facing the Palace Green. It is named for Elkanah Deane, a prosperous Colonial coachmaker. Although the historic corner fence, once used to discourage too-close clipping of corners by carriages, has been revived in Williamsburg, its use is now largely decorative. The facade of this house bears a close resemblance to that of the neighboring Carter-Saunders House.

The first of the Craft Shops we encounter is the DEANE SHOP AND FORGE on Prince George Street. Here a skilled craftsman will be found, cheerfully fashioning wrought iron objects with 18th Century implements.

The DEANE SHOP AND FORGE and its elongated covered wagon become part of a highly pictorial composition when viewed from the west across a shallow ravine. The zig-zag rail fence adds to the frontier flavor.

The last building on the left before we reach the Governor's Palace is the CARTER - SAUNDERS HOUSE, a restored hip-roofed dwelling dating from before 1746. Governor Dinwiddie lived here while the Palace was being repaired in 1751. It derived its name from Robert Carter of Nomini Hall, a member of the Council who purchased it in 1761. He sold it around 1801 to Robert Saunders, President of the College of William and Mary.

The doorway (right) has an individual pedimented shelter, unsupported by columns.

One of the more subtle fascinations of Williamsburg consists of the play of sunlight on its whitewashed walls. Such a pleasant pattern of light occupies the foreground of this view of the CARTER-SAUNDERS GARDEN, while the forms of the Palace Buildings loom through the foliage beyond the picket fence. These gardens, shaded by ancient trees, are among the loveliest in the city.

One of Williamsburg's most picturesque and unconventional thoroughfares is Scotland Path. It approaches the Palace Green from the west, between hedges of blossoms, and provides glimpses of the Palace Gardens.

Williamsburg's varied fences and garden gates form the subject of an architectural essay all by themselves. This picket fence encloses the garden of the CARTER-SAUNDERS HOUSE. Beyond it lies the Governor's Palace.

The beauty and expanse of the wide PALACE GREEN can best be appreciated from a vantage point on the roof of the Governor's Palace.

The Governor's Palace

The culminating architectural achievement of the restoration is this magnificent residence of the Royal Governors which was the center of social life in Virginia during three-quarters of the 18th Century. After many delays, work was begun on the original structure in 1706, during Governor Nott's term of office. At that time £3000 was appropriated to build a suitable estate, but the project proved far costlier than this. The Burgesses soon began to complain about the high-handed manner in which the Governor lavished the public's money, and the townspeople soon referred to it sarcastically as the "Palace," a term which later became accepted. In subsequent years, when the cry of extravagance had died down somewhat, the elaborate "Ball-Room Wing" was added, making this a residence unparalleled for luxury in the Colonies. A succession of Royal Governors, most of them on excellent terms with the populace, resided here, until the tension immediately preceding the Revolution forced the departure of Governor Dunmore. Thereafter it served as the home of the first two Governors of the Commonwealth, Patrick Henry and Thomas Jefferson. The latter, being architecturally minded, jotted down floor plans of the

building which were of great help to Colonial Williamsburg more than a century and a half later. At the time of the Yorktown Campaign the Governor's Palace served as a hospital for the wounded, during which occupancy it was destroyed by fire in 1781. Two flanking buildings, the Guard House and the Governor's Office, survived however, and were used as private dwellings until 1863, when they were torn down by Union soldiers.

The Governor's Palace and its Gardens have been restored with complete authenticity, by virtue of the generous funds available and the scholarly and thoroughgoing research undertaken by the architects and historians. This research was facilitated by ample records, inventories, family letters and archaeological remains. In addition to Thomas Jefferson's careful sketches, the elevation on the Bodleian plate and details of the "Frenchman's Map" were of primary assistance. After removing the modern High School building which stood on the site, the excavators were able to find the actual foundation walls and stone basement floors of the original building.

At the far end of the Palace Green is the formal entrance to THE GOVERNOR'S PALACE, an imposing iron-grilled gate whose brick supporting posts are topped with the British Lion and Unicorn. Beyond the low curving brick wall the path leads through a formal forecourt to the stately white portal of the Palace, surmounted by a wrought iron balcony.

The facade of the GOVERNOR'S PALACE is conceived in the early Georgian style. Its two ample stories are surmounted with a steep hip roof and a lantern cupola, flanked with two generous Tidewater Virginia chimneys. Lanterns were lighted in this cupola to celebrate the King's birthday and other noteworthy events.

The long tranquil PALACE GREEN has a simple pastoral quality, not entirely dispelled by the dignified symbol of Royal prestige which faces its northern extremity. A few privileged cows have grazed here in times past.

A drypoint of the GOVERNOR'S PALACE, made in the first flush of Spring, emphasizes the airiness and grace of the buildings at the end of the Palace Green. The narrow, many-paned windows and dormers are subtly spaced.

Visitors leave the Palace Gardens through this formal pedimented gateway to the West yard.

There are many evidences of the fine furnishings which graced the GOVERNOR'S PALACE in Colonial days. In addition to the "standing furniture," each Royal Governor brought a large collection of his own. In the Parlor is an old marble fireplace of unusual interest. Excavators found the original carved central marble panel sufficiently intact to be used here. Over it hangs an 18th Century flower painting. The chandelier is from the same period and the fine old carpet dates from about 1725.

The Little Dining Room of the GOVERNOR'S PALACE was used by the Governor and his family. On the mantel-piece are five pieces of Whieldon Agate Ware. Several grates of the type shown in the fireplace were brought over by successive Governors. The Queen Anne tea table, an American piece, is cherished by collectors.

The Supper Room of the GOVERNOR'S PALACE strongly reflects the Chinese influence. The chandelier was once used in the East India House in Canton and the old wall paper was painted by hand in China for an 18th Century English house. The Queen Anne corner cupboard and the pediment of the doorway both show the Oriental trend.

In 1749 repairs were ordered for the GOVERNOR'S PALACE, and the Ballroom was probably added in 1751. It now contains a fine old harpsichord and two notable portraits of Queen Catherine of Braganza and Charles II.

In the Bed Chamber over the Dining Room of the GOVERNOR'S PALACE is a very early 17th Century bed with Crewel work hangings. Around the Queen Anne walnut table are four yew wood chairs carved to resemble bamboo. Old Delft tiles line the fireplace opening and the panelled woodwork is painted an oyster-shell white.

(Left) In the service courtyard is the Kitchen of the GOVERNOR'S PALACE, which contains ladles, forks, trivets, toasters, skewers, waffle irons, kettles and other quaint accessories needed for fireplace cookery.

The West Yard of the GOVERNOR'S PALACE, complete with kitchen, scullery, smoke house, laundry, dairy, well and salthouse, was the scene of feverish animation on banquet nights. Serving an elaborate dinner across the courtyard involved as much of a strain upon the stamina of the servants as upon the purse of the Governor.

Two pictures of the Salt House and Smokehouse of the GOVERNOR'S PALACE show the mellowing effect of the weather upon whitewashed clapboards. The view on the left was taken eight years later than that on the right.

No less than ten distinct gardens are incorporated in the elaborate landscaping of the GOVERNOR'S PALACE. Most of them are conventional, but informal corners of great charm can be sought out by the unhurried explorer.

The intricate pattern of the Ballroom Garden is well defined when observed from the roof of the GOVERNOR'S PALACE. Hedges were popular in Colonial days in Virginia, particularly boxwood, which grew slowly and did not require frequent clipping. In the background is the North Garden, gay with flowers and flanked by an arbor leading to the corner pavilion.

(Right) Rooftop view of the East Yard.

The Ballroom wing of the GOVERNOR'S PALACE and the formal planting of the Palace Gardens are brought out in this drypoint. Only trees, shrubs and flowers known to be current in Colonial days are found in this garden.

A vista through the decorative North Gates of the PALACE GARDENS. Careful research into a wide range of documents on both sides of the Atlantic has made possible such a trustworthy glimpse of Colonial grandeur.

A familiar garden view of the GOVERNOR'S PALACE shows that the principal building was nearly square in plan before the Ballroom wing was added in 1751.

The formality of the gardens of the GOVERNOR'S PALACE is enhanced by graceful iron gates. Near this spot a giant willow marks the common grave of 156 Revolutionary soldiers whose unidentified remains were uncovered during the recent restoration.

The gable end of the Ballroom extension of the GOVERNOR'S PALACE is embellished with a colorful painted wood carving of the Royal Arms of George II. This wing was added in 1751, but few repairs appear to have been made in succeeding years. By 1781 the Palace was said to show "signs of grandeur, but in a ruinous condition."

From a tree-sheltered retreat on "The Mount" the visitor obtains a fine view of the intricacies of the MAZE, a complex puzzle in clipped holly hedges in the old English tradition. The Palace looms in the distance.

The CANAL and GOVERNOR'S FISH POND, a narrow body of water at the western extremity of the Palace Gardens, was largely restored by rebuilding an old dam. It is now encircled by a foot path for the more leisurely visitor.

The architectural style of the pavilions, or "necessary houses," which occupy far corners of the North Garden of the GOVERNOR'S PALACE is matched by their utility. The location of brick walls was verified by uncovering long forgotten foundations.

(Right) The formal gates which enclose the North Garden of the GOVERNOR'S PALACE are richly Georgian in character.

Decorative wrought iron gates make a pleasantly ornate frame for the GOVERNOR'S PALACE.

After the splendor of the Governor's Palace, the BRUSH HOUSE, its neighbor at the northeast corner of the Palace Green, seems modest indeed. The house was built by John Brush, gunsmith and keeper of the Powder Magazine, between 1717 and 1719. These two photographs reveal the typical condition of an old Williamsburg house before restoration. The handsome and extensive boxwood gardens of the BRUSH HOUSE are reputed to be the oldest in Williamsburg, and are open to the public.

The path which borders the Palace Green on the east passes an open lot which was once occupied by the FIRST THEATRE IN AMERICA, built ca. 1716. At the right is the Levingston House, originally built at the same time.

This little steep-roofed, grey and white house facing the Palace Green was the home of William Levingston, who built the first playhouse in the Colonies on a site adjoining his home.

One of the new projects of Colonial Williamsburg will be the rebuilding of the old theatre, the first in America, which stood on the site just north of the Levingston House. Here will be revived some of the plays which were favorites in Colonial days. The site was given by Mr. George P. Coleman.

One of the most beautiful of Williamsburg residences, the ST. GEORGE TUCKER HOUSE, has had a pronounced influence upon American house design. Its facade on Nicholson Street reveals a subtle unbalanced symmetry.

Seen from the west across billowy clumps of boxwood, the wings of the ST. GEORGE TUCKER HOUSE pile up picturesquely. The chimney of the kitchen stands a few inches away from the gable to reduce the risk of fire.

A drypoint of the St. George Tucker House. This building was bought by St. George Tucker in 1788, who then enlarged it to its present size. Tucker, a native of Bermuda, first came to Williamsburg to enter the College of William and Mary. Later he studied law with George Wythe, becoming his clerk and finally his successor as professor of law at the College. In addition, Tucker was a poet and dramatist of note. A long line of his distinguished descendents have lived in this house.

On a March morning the St. George Tucker House appears dwarfed by large trees. The one in the right foreground has since disappeared. In Spring the tulip garden on this property is Williamsburg's most colorful spot.

Although built in the early Republican period, the St. George Tucker House possesses the distinction and simplicity of earlier days. There is a pleasant irregularity to the clapboards and the window spacing.

A detail of the facade of the St. George Tucker House. Its early owner is supposed to have installed the first bath tub in Williamsburg in his garden, filling the tub by means of a pipe from the well house. Here also the first Christmas tree in Williamsburg was set up in 1842, a tradition which has been carried on ever since.

(Right) The St. George Tucker House makes a picture from many informal angles.

Our path along Nicholson Street leads past two dignified white houses facing the Market Square: the ARCHIBALD BLAIR HOUSE, built between 1716 and 1718, and the RANDOLPH-PEACHY HOUSE, whose steep-roofed wing has recently been reconstructed. This house was built about 1715. In 1724 it was bought by Sir John Randolph, able lawyer and economist, and the only native Virginian to be knighted. As Virginia's representative in London, Randolph did much to bring prosperity to Colonial tobacco growers. He bequeathed the house to his distinguished son, Peyton Randolph, first President of the First Continental Congress. Two famous generals, Lafayette and Rochambeau, made their headquarters here before the Siege of Yorktown. Lafayette returned to be entertained in this house on his memorable trip to America in 1824. The unusual length of the house is due to the fact that it was formed by joining two houses together.

(Left) Detail of the facade of the RANDOLPH-PEACHY HOUSE.

The Archibald Blair House as it appeared in 1936, with a glimpse of the Randolph-Peachy House at the right. The planting of the restored areas of Williamsburg is now less prodigal.

The restored dairy of the Archibald Blair House is but one of scores of similar structures which have been replaced or restored by Colonial Williamsburg. Many of them have been adapted as guest houses.

Our path now turns back upon itself, providing one of the unexpected vistas which occur so often in Williamsburg. This one shows the steeple of Bruton Parish Church looming beyond the stable of the Geddy House.

A pencil drawing of the outbuildings and garden of the JAMES GEDDY HOUSE. This is one of the six smaller gardens which are open to the public without charge.

At the southern end of the Palace Green is the JAMES GEDDY HOUSE, an original frame structure with a steep-roofed wing. It was built by James Geddy, gunsmith and jeweler, whose shop probably faced the Palace Green.

The JAMES GEDDY HOUSE is one of the few in Williamsburg to possess an elaborate entrance porch.

The white outbuildings of the JAMES GEDDY HOUSE become more visible with the fall of Autumn leaves.

The Norton House, a pleasant brick structure just west of the Old Court House, has changed hands many times. Its owners included a watchmaker, a gunsmith and silversmith, a tailor and tavern keeper, a merchant, a surgeon and a schoolmaster. It was acquired in 1778 by John Hatley Norton, Virginia representative of his father's famous mercantile firm in London. Here he lived with his wife Sally, daughter of Robert Carter Nicholas, Treasurer of the Colony. The sculptor who carved the statue of Lord Botetourt was commissioned through this firm, and the tea which was thrown overboard by the Patriots at Yorktown had been ordered by the same house.

Set in the center of the Market Square is the OLD COURT HOUSE, a well proportioned little brick building with a cupola. It was built in 1770 to serve the administrative needs both of the City of Williamsburg and James City County. Gutted by fire in 1911 and then rebuilt, it was finally restored in 1932. The building of a modern Court House on England Street has freed this historic structure for use as a museum. Its chief exhibits are the noteworthy Archaeological Exhibition of Colonial Williamsburg, together with photographs and documents, among them the famous Bodleian copper plate and a facsimile of the "Frenchman's Map." The museum, which also serves as an information center, is open to the public free of charge.

The portico of the OLD COURT HOUSE is a cantilevered gabled hood for which columns were intended but never arrived. Columns were added after the fire of 1911, but they have now been sacrificed for authenticity.

Market Square, framed in one of its superb wine glass elms.

A detail of the OLD COURT HOUSE.

The old brick walk leads up the Duke of Gloucester Street past the OLD COURT HOUSE to the newly painted brightness of CHOWNING'S TAVERN.

The T-shaped plan of the OLD COURT HOUSE is apparent when viewed from the north side of the Market Square. In the distance, beyond the Powder Magazine, is the new James City Court House.

This cheerful little building on the Market Square is CHOWNING'S TAVERN, an alehouse where the traveler may now stop for rest and refreshment just as his counterpart did in the 18th Century.

The shop sign of CHOWNING'S TAVERN consists of a tankard receiving a decorative cascade of liquid.

A glimpse of the well and the hand-hewn picket fence behind CHOWNING'S TAVERN.

Autumn foliage casts sweeping shadows across the clapboards of Josiah Chowning's Tavern. This building stands on the site of the rambling Williamsburg Inn Annex, mention of which evokes pleasant memories for many early visitors to the restored capital.

BLAIR'S BRICK HOUSE, a reconstructed dwelling, is occupied by a very tempting antique shop. Its handsome gardens, which connect with those of the Ludwell-Paradise House, are open to the public.

The Ludwell-Paradise House

Behind the dignified, almost austere facade of this brick dwelling on the Duke of Gloucester Street lies a history filled with several unconventional chapters. The house was built about 1717 by Philip Ludwell II, one of the wealthiest planters and most influential men in the Colonies. When only twenty-three he was elected Speaker of the House of Burgesses. The house is typical of the more pretentious Colonial "town house," and was probably used by the Ludwells during "Publick Times."

It was inherited by Philip Ludwell III who, in turn, willed it to his eldest daughter and her husband, William Lee. The house is more popularly associated with the name of his second daughter Lucy, wife of John Paradise, a scholarly Londoner and close friend of Dr. Samuel Johnson. The Paradises spent much time in London, where their home became something of a social center for American sympathizers during the Rev-

olution, and where Lucy Ludwell Paradise startled society by her eccentric behavior. She once poured scalding tea on a London gentleman who displeased her. In 1805, when she returned to live in this house as a widow, she installed her coach in a hall at the rear of the house. She was in the habit of receiving her guests in this coach, while servants rolled it back and forth. Finally her caprices became so eccentric that she was committed to a lunatic hospital, where she died in 1814. Litigation over her estate brought her grandson, Count Philip Barziza, to Williamsburg from Venice. Although much of his time was occupied in fruitless lawsuits, he was actively engaged in other ways. He and his wife managed to produce ten children in Williamsburg, the last of whom was known as Decimus Ultimus Barziza.

The Ludwell-Paradise House is now open to the public, and houses the unique collection of American Folk Art assembled by Mrs. John D. Rockefeller, Jr.

The LUDWELL-PARADISE HOUSE, soundly built and well preserved, required little restoration. The basket weave effect of the Flemish bond brickwork, accented with glazed headers, is noticeable on the upper story.

A side view of the LUDWELL-PARADISE HOUSE reveals the peculiar lean-to construction which enlarged the ground floor to a depth of two rooms and still preserved cross ventilation in the second-story bedrooms.

The public is invited to wander through the box-bordered brick paths of the LUDWELL-PARADISE gardens. Here the well cover, the smokehouse and the white frame kitchen have all been rebuilt where they once stood. There are welcome benches here for the footweary.

(Right) An unconventional view of the LUDWELL-PARADISE HOUSE from Nicholson Street. For those who wonder whether football or dice is the impelling motive in the foreground group, the answer is—football.

The cheerful stable of the LUDWELL-PARADISE HOUSE has been rebuilt upon its old foundations. It provides attractive accommodations for pigeons, as well as for horses and carriages built on 18th Century lines.

Beyond the smokehouse is a glimpse of the lean-to of the LUDWELL-PARADISE HOUSE.

Another view of the brick and frame stable of the LUDWELL-PARADISE HOUSE in early autumn.

A few old unrestored houses in Williamsburg have retained their Colonial character so well that they now fit handsomely into the picture of the revived 18th Century town. The TAYLOE HOUSE is one of these. A gambrel-roofed house of great charm, it looks across Nicholson Street to the gardens of the Ludwell-Paradise House.

A few steps from the Ludwell-Paradise House is the BARBER AND PERUKE MAKER'S SHOP, where the visitor can obtain an excellent idea of the tonsorial treatment he could have expected in Colonial days. The shop, which contains a rare collection of 18th Century barber shop prints, wigs and perukes, scissors and irons, is open to the public free of charge.

Across the generous width of the Duke of Gloucester Street, these small buildings appear sedate and somewhat dwarfed in scale. There is a tradition that the little brick building with a swag roof, now the shop of the Wig Maker, was once one of the early drug stores in America and known as the "Unicorn's Horn." The famous shipment of tea thrown overboard at the "Yorktown Tea Party" in 1774 was consigned to this shop, at that time occupied by Prentis and Company.

These are the establishments of two apothecaries. The BARBER AND PERUKE MAKER'S SHOP at the left occupies the building which originally was Dr. Blair's Apothecary Shop. Adjoining it is the home of Dr. George Pitt, whose small druggist's shop was known as the "Sign of the Rhinoceros."

Another view of the same subject as above, taken during the enchanted fortnight when the dogwood is in full bloom. At the right is the site of the Printing Office of the "Virginia Gazette," the oldest newspaper in Virginia.

A pen-and-ink sketch of a shaded segment of the DUKE OF GLOUCESTER STREET shows, in the center, the apothecary's shop built by the locally celebrated Dr. Archibald Blair, and occupied by him and his descendents during most of the 18th Century.

After passing the original site of the Printing Office of the Virginia Gazette, the brick path leads to the TETERAL SHOP, shown on the left. This served for many years as a general store, and is now a drugstore.

The camera points westward on a Springtime afternoon to record the shimmering clapboards and nearly perpendicular gambrel roof of the WATERS-COLEMAN HOUSE. Henry Gill, who served three terms as Mayor of Williamsburg, lived here.

(Right) The adjoining store is THE DAVIDSON SHOP, occupied around 1737 by Dr. Robert Davidson, Mayor of Williamsburg and "Doctor of Physic." Here the good doctor kept an apothecary's shop during the first quarter of the 18th Century, where he sold "all sorts of Balsams, Decoctions, Electuaries, Elixirs, Emplaisters, Extracts, Infusions, Liquors, Magisteries, Oils and Ointments."

This early view of the DAVIDSON SHOP shows tempting Smithfield hams in the windows and thick corn husk mats for sale on the front steps.

John Brooke, an innkeeper, began construction of the long narrow PRENTIS HOUSE between 1712 and 1714, and willed the property to his daughter and her husband William Prentis, one of a long line of Williamsburg merchants. Their son, John Prentis, was Mayor in 1768, and a Colonel of the Militia.

Adjoining the garden of the PRENTIS HOUSE is a covered well of unusual charm. The picket fence is one of more than thirty types which can be found in restored Williamsburg. A ball weight on a chain closes the gate.

The SIGN OF THE GOLDEN BALL offers a shaded bench to the passerby as well as a lesson in metal working.

The sunny outbuildings of the SIGN OF THE GOLDEN BALL border on the west courtyard of the Raleigh Tavern.

The Sign of the Golden Ball—This little Colonial building has had an active commercial career. In 1775 it flourished as Dr. George Gilmer's Apothecary Shop. Before the recent restoration the passing motorist stopped here to have his "flats fixed," and now it serves as the Craft Shop of a skilled pewterer who demonstrates his art to visitors who are interested.

There are a few rare days in Springtime when the SIGN OF THE GOLDEN BALL can be partially framed in full blooming dogwood. This photograph is taken from the site of the old King's Arms Tavern.

The Raleigh Tavern

This, the most famous of Virginia taverns, was truly an extraordinary institution, playing a momentous role in the early history of the Colonies. It was a place of entertainment and good refreshment, a traditional center of social activity and political intrigue, an informal meeting place of the most celebrated Virginians. Among its early guests were Washington, Jefferson, Patrick Henry, Lafayette and Rochambeau, along with many lesser statesmen and soldiers, and perhaps a few rogues and adventurers. Williamsburg boasted 25 or 30 taverns, inns and ordinaries in Colonial days, some more snobbish, some less expensive than the RALEIGH, but none of them possessing its prestige or elegance, or its significance in Colonial affairs.

In its handsome, blue-panelled Apollo room the gentry of the Colony joined military officers and college students in dancing the minuet and the quadrille. But not all the happenings in the Apollo were frivolous.

In 1769, when the Royal Governor dissolved the House of Burgesses and locked its members out of the Capitol, they promptly met here and adopted the Non-Importation agreement. Here it was decided to call the Continental Congress, at whose third meeting the Declaration of Independence was signed. Truly a spark of the Revolution was kindled in the RALEIGH TAVERN. When the youthful, red-headed Thomas Jefferson came to Williamsburg to seek the good graces of the bewitching young Rebecca Burwell of Carter's Grove, he danced with her in the Apollo room. She was the belle of Williamsburg and the idol of the college students, who called her the "Fair Belinda." Later she married not Jefferson, but his friend Jacquelin Ambler, and when Jefferson returned, it was not as a suitor but as a serious leader of the House of Burgesses and later as the Governor of the new Republican state of Virginia.

Phi Beta Kappa, the first Greek letter honor society in America, was founded in December 1776 by a group of students of the College of William and Mary, and there is a well founded tradition that they first met in the Apollo Room of the RALEIGH TAVERN to establish their society.

The TAVERN was built sometime before 1742, possibly as early as 1710. At the peak of its popularity, prior to the Revolution, its public rooms included the famous Apollo, the Daphne, a parlor, dining room, gaming room and bar. These rooms are accurately recreated and refurnished in the present structure, which rises on its old foundations, a most authentic replica of the original building.

A prodigious amount of data has enabled the research staff to be accurate down to the smallest details, and even to point out errors in an on-the-spot sketch made by Benson J. Lossing for his "Field Book of the Revolution."

The old hostelry remained active for many years after the Revolution, even when the Capitol was transferred to Richmond in 1780. Lafayette was banqueted here during the course of his return trip to America in 1824. Its last notable guest was probably President Tyler, who attended a banquet in his honor in 1859. In December of that year the RALEIGH TAVERN burned to the ground, shortly after another serious fire had damaged the Wren Building.

The RALEIGH TAVERN became the accepted meeting place for planters, traders, adventurers and merchants who strolled down this path to complete their transactions over a pipe of tobacco or a mug of ale in the Raleigh bar.

The street facade of the L-shaped RALEIGH TAVERN is cheerful and inviting, faced with white weatherboards which shimmer in the sunlight. Over the main doorway is the leaden bust of Sir Walter Raleigh.

The long west facade of the RALEIGH TAVERN is brightened by an even dozen dormer windows. This wing, which contains the famous Apollo and Daphne Rooms, was built upon the old foundations uncovered in 1928.

The sidewalk in front of the RALEIGH TAVERN was a scene of noisy animation on auction days when slaves, coaches, horses, cattle, prize ships or confiscated Loyalist property would be sold to the highest bidder.

The facade of the RALEIGH TAVERN responds brightly to the clear sunshine of early spring.

The RALEIGH TAVERN seen through a pink and white screen of dogwood in bloom.

The unusually large kitchen wing of the RALEIGH TAVERN looks out upon a small formal garden. A new name was added to the list of distinguished guests of the Tavern when Winston Churchill had tea here in 1946.

An early view of the rebuilt RALEIGH TAVERN, taken from the opposite side of the Duke of Gloucester Street, shows two facades and seventeen dormers. Two modern brick buildings stood on this site before the restoration.

An old well occupies a central spot in the garden of the RALEIGH TAVERN. However, this hospitable inn was much better known for its good food, Arrack punch and "exceeding good Madeira" than for its drinking water.

A corner of the celebrated Green Parlor of the RALEIGH TAVERN contains a fine old cherry wood secretary which came originally from Virginia. The wing chair is covered with colorful Crewel work. The very detailed inventories left by successive Colonial landlords have made it possible to furnish the Tavern rooms authentically.

The bar of the RALEIGH TAVERN is an inviting room with a corner fireplace panelled in natural pine where businessmen, bon vivants and army officers of the time gathered over pewter mugs. Its hard wood furniture is robustly made, to stand hard usage. Henry Wetherburn, the first known landlord of the TAVERN, was famous for the Arrack punch he dispensed here. He later left the RALEIGH and acquired three other taverns by the expedient of marrying their keeper's widows. There is no mention of bigamy in the records and Henry Wetherburn deserves great credit for his achievement in thus becoming the owner of one of the first "hotel chains."

The bar (right) was really barred in this instance, being so arranged that the bartender could pull down his wooden wicket to protect his stock of bottles during brief absences in the wine cellar.

In his diaries, George Washington frequently mentions dining in the Daphne Room, the private dining room of the RALEIGH TAVERN. Its appointments are luxurious. Gold damask curtains frame the windows. The original of the wall paper, which follows a Chinese design, was found serving as a cover for the old court records of Southhampton County. The three-part mahogany table is surrounded by six old English chairs, while two fine walnut cellarets flank the fireplace. On the sideboard are two antique mahogany knife cases.

The famous powder-blue Apollo Room of the RALEIGH TAVERN was the legendary setting of important meetings in Williamsburg, and a center of social life surpassed only by the Governor's Palace. On many a gay evening it lived up to the motto carved over its fireplace: HILARITAS SAPIENTIAE ET BONAE VITAE PROLES, which can be translated as "Jollity is the offspring of wisdom and good living."

(Right) A more informal atmosphere pervades the public dining room of the RALEIGH TAVERN. The framed map over the fireplace is the one carried by Lafayette during his campaign.

In Colonial days the eastern end of the Duke of Gloucester Street was studded with convivial inns. On the site of the RED LION INN this smiling white house has been built. The Red Lion, constructed about 1719, contained the shop of a wig maker and hair dresser, and had a brick kitchen and a billiard house in the back yard.

An excellent example of a fine old Williamsburg residence before restoration is the LEE HOUSE, standing a few doors east of the Raleigh Tavern. Restoring this weather-beaten house is an early project of Colonial Williamsburg. A famous inn stood on this site in 1717.

(Right) The double chimneys of the reconstructed ALEXANDER CRAIG HOUSE rise up over the Raleigh Tavern's garden fence.

BURDETTE'S ORDINARY was one in a cluster of inns which grew up close to the Capitol. As a result of a lawsuit between the owner of this ordinary and its neighbor, the Red Lion, sketches were made of the two buildings. These show that Burdette's Ordinary was one of the few Williamsburg buildings to possess an extended porch chamber. Our path now leads through the west garden of the Raleigh Tavern to the Old Gaol.

The Old Gaol

The original gaol was built at about the same time as the Capitol, and in close proximity to it. Henry Cary, Williamsburg's master builder, began work on its heavy brick walls in 1701, and by 1704 the building was ready to begin its bleak career as Virginia's first penitentiary. For the next two centuries it served as a prison, first for the Colony and Commonwealth and finally as a City Jail. Some of the original walls remained when the City deeded it to Colonial Williamsburg in 1933. It has been restored to its appearance of 1773 and is far more pleasant to contemplate now than in the days when its hapless inmates languished in irons on malodorous straw.

The OLD GAOL was first intended for prisoners awaiting trial before the General Court in the Capitol. Confinement was not for long periods, for the Court usually specified quick and violent punishment, such as lashing, branding or hanging. Thus the cost of maintaining prisoners was reduced and the prison would be emptied for a new batch of inmates. The death penalty was handed out rather freely, since forgery, horse stealing and burglary were capital offenses at that time. During the winter months the prisoners suffered intensely from the cold in their unheated cells. Crowded in together, with handcuffs and leg irons riveted on and with a fare consisting of "salt beef damaged and Indian meal," their lot was truly a miserable one. Few of them would have agreed with the Rev. Hugh Jones that it was "a strong sweet Prison for Criminals."

Williamsburg had its share of lawless elements—newly arrived, half savage slaves, felonious servants, adventurers, pirates and marauding Indians. All these found their way into the OLD GAOL. Perhaps the most distinguished ruffians of the lot were thirteen members of Black Beard's piratical crew who were thrown into this pestilential hole in 1718 and later marched to the gallows in Capitol Landing Road. During the Revolution the cells were thronged with traitors, Tories, deserters and spies.

Seen between picturesque haystacks at sunset, the OLD GAOL possesses an almost idyllic quality which was not appreciated by its miserable prisoners in the grim 18th Century days. The Capitol looms up in the background.

Portions of the original brickwork are evident in the north wall of the OLD GAOL. The prisoners did not exercise in this generous garden enclosed with palings, but in a tiny courtyard behind the wall.

The Keeper's quarters occupy most of the front wing of the L-shaped OLD GAOL. Here lived the last and most colorful Colonial keeper, Peter Pelham, who also served as organist of Bruton Church and taught refined young ladies to become proficient at the harpsichord and spinet. Pelham was suspected of connivance in permitting prisoners to escape from the gaol, but his name was cleared after an investigation ordered by the Assembly.

Two sombre windows penetrated the thick brick walls of the original building of the OLD GAOL completed in 1704. They were covered with thick iron grates, but were unglazed, making the cells so cold in winter that deaths from freezing were frequent.

Reproductions of the old pillory and stocks now stand before the courtyard of the OLD GAOL. Persons who found themselves imprisoned in these sadistic contraptions were often pelted by the public in Colonial days. Both devices are now in incessant demand by amateur photographers.

The serene hilltop behind the OLD GAOL is studded with rows of haystacks formed about center poles in the 18th Century manner.

The original Keeper's quarters in the corner room of the OLD GAOL was transformed into a Debtor's Cell after 1722. The sanitary arrangements seem crude now, but were considered quite advanced at that time.

The rambling old COKE-GARRETT HOUSE, dating from the early part of the 18th Century, was the home of John Coke, silversmith and jeweler. During the Revolution it was run as a tavern by his widow. Its landscaped gardens now are second only to those of the Governor's Palace in beauty.

A Spring lane, bordered with blossoms, leads to the 19th Century farm buildings of the old ROBERT WALLER property. Williamsburg rewards the inquisitive wanderer with many vistas such as this.

The house of DR. ROBERT WALLER, its double porch facing the east wing of the Capitol, dates from the mid-18th Century. The classic cottage in the foreground belonged to the same property.

Another Williamsburg house which has left its mark on present day domestic architecture is the SEMPLE HOUSE, which faces the Capitol on Francis Street. This restrained and dignified dwelling reflects the best in the early Federal style. Its white frame gable faces the street, flanked by two symmetrical wings. The exact date of its construction is not known. Judge James Semple, professor of law at the College of William and Mary, lived here as early as 1799. The house remained in his family until 1850.

The reposeful SEMPLE HOUSE sits securely behind its picket fence and looks out on the world from a lush frame of vegetation. For many years this was mistakenly thought to be the home of Peyton Randolph.

In Springtime the kitchen of the SEMPLE HOUSE is becomingly screened by dogwood blossoms.

The garden facade of the SEMPLE HOUSE possesses the same graceful dignity which characterizes its street elevation. There is a pronounced difference between the heights of the first and second story windows.

One of Williamsburg's most beautifully carved porches graces the SEMPLE HOUSE.

The garden path offers a sharp perspective of the south facade of the SEMPLE HOUSE.

One of the oldest unrestored buildings in Virginia is the WILLIAM ROBERTSON HOUSE, near the Capitol on Francis Street. It is possible that only the Wren Building is older in Williamsburg. The house was probably built by William Robertson about 1709 and was sold to John Grymes of Middlesex in 1723. It became the possession of the Galt family in the late 19th Century. Steep-roofed, authentic and commodious, it harmonizes well with the restored community which adjoins it.

(Left) Detail of the ROBERTSON HOUSE.

AYSCOUGH'S SHOP—In 1768, when Governor Fauquier bestowed a generous bequest upon his faithful cook, Ann Ayscough and her husband Christopher, who worked in the Palace Gardens, they invested their reward in a tavern on this desirable site close to the Capitol.

17

A side view of AYSCOUGH'S SHOP reveals its peculiar sloping roof line and pedimented well house. This is one of the six Craft Shops operated by Colonial Williamsburg, and is open to the public without admission charge.

AYSCOUGH'S SHOP now serves as a workshop for skilled cabinet makers who wear Colonial costumes and employ 18th Century implements in restoring and repairing furniture used in the exhibition buildings.

The Capitol

Balancing the Wren Building at the other end of the Duke of Gloucester Street, THE CAPITOL stood for several decades as a symbol of loyalty to the King. Later it represented Colonial discontent and finally it became the birthplace of the Virginia Commonwealth. Perhaps the most significant of Williamsburg buildings, it has been recreated with convincing accuracy exactly as it was until 1747. The original building was erected between 1701 and 1705 under the "overseership" of Henry Cary. Here was held the General Assembly of Virginia, the Governor's Council and the General Court. In 1747 the original Capitol was destroyed by a disastrous fire. A new structure of a more classical design had supplanted it by 1753. During the troubled days preceding the Revolution these walls rang with unforgettable words. In the House of Burgesses rose young Patrick Henry to attack the Stamp Act and to issue his famous warning to George III. Here Thomas Jefferson obtained religious freedom for his state and George Mason presented the first Bill of Rights. When Governor Dunmore fled to a British warship in the York River, this salmon-pink brick building became the birthplace of the new Republican State.

Its decline began when the seat of government was changed to Richmond in 1780. For a time it was used by Judge George Wythe to hold moot courts. Later it served as a Court of Admiralty, then a law school, military hospital and grammar school. By 1794 it was in such a sad state of repair that half of the building was torn down to provide for the upkeep of the other half. In 1832 the remainder of the structure was burned to the ground. Its site and old foundations were conserved by the Association for the Preservation of Virginia Antiquities, however.

This Society turned the site over to Colonial Williamsburg, and work was begun on the present structure in 1930, to be finished in 1934. Working from meticulous and detailed records, the builders have been able to make a virtual counterpart of the original structure which first rose on these same foundations in 1705. Two examples will illustrate the extraordinary precautions taken to assure authenticity. To obtain the original Purbeck stone used in the paving of the Court Chamber, the old quarry in England from which it came was temporarily reopened. The crown glass of the windows in THE CAPITOL was ordered from the same factory in England which produced the original glass over 200 years ago.

The CAPITOL, which the camera has caught here behind a springtime screen of paper mulberry branches, is an H-shaped building with circular bays. Two previous capitol buildings have stood on these same foundations.

An unconventional view of the CAPITOL, partly hidden by Christopher Ayscough's outbuildings. During "Publick Times" the Burgesses were only a short stroll away from a mug of ale at Ayscough's hospitable tavern.

A detailed view of one of the most significant buildings in Colonial America. Under the arcade which connects the two main elements of the CAPITOL once stood the marble statue of the much respected Royal Governor, Lord Botetourt.

Pencil drawing of the CAPITOL. The graceful white cupola bears the arms of Queen Anne, during whose reign the first Capitol was erected. This is surmounted by a clock, and above this flies the "Great Union," Britain's flag in Colonial days.

The total absence of chimneys on the CAPITOL can be observed from this vantage point. Neither smoking nor fire of any kind was at first permitted, and the original building was purposely built without chimneys.

The COUNCIL CHAMBER—In this stately oval room the Royal Governor met with his Council. This was the upper house of the Assembly, corresponding to the House of Lords in England. Its architectural treatment, therefore, was more elegant than that of the Hall of the Burgesses. Around the oval table are grouped fourteen Jacobean chairs, just as they were in the early 18th Century. Between marbleized pilasters the portrait of Queen Anne and the Royal Arms look down upon the Councillors. The extra long green baize table cloth made a welcome lap robe during cold winter sessions in the unheated chamber.

In the Office of the Clerk of the House of Burgesses hangs a full length portrait of George Washington by Charles Willson Peale, a replica of one in Philadelphia, and one of fourteen Washington portraits painted by this artist. This one was Washington's favorite, and he presented it to a friend living at Shirley, the old estate on the James River. The Father of His Country had good reason to remember the Capitol, since it was here that he stood, blushing and confused, while the Speaker paid public tribute to his "brave and steady behavior" in the French and Indian War.

The COURT CHAMBER—In this handsome panelled room was held the General Court, highest in the Colony, where the Governor and his Council heard civil and criminal cases and appeals. The spectators were relegated to a very limited space in the suspended gallery at the left.

The HOUSE OF BURGESSES, the people's representatives, convened in the East wing of the Capitol. The original Speaker's chair, with its cabriole legs and panelled back, occupies the center of the circular wall.

The tortured silhouette of a paper mulberry tree forms an unconventional frame for the CAPITOL which the Reverend Hugh Jones, in the 18th Century called "a noble, beautiful, and commodious Pile as any of its Kind."

Marking the eastern extremity of the Duke of Gloucester Street, which is seven-eights of a mile long, is the side gateway of the Capitol. Beyond the open gates is the KERR HOUSE, a dignified, vine-covered brick mansion which once served as McClelland's Headquarters. Alexander Kerr occupied it from 1732 until his death in 1738. It was enlarged shortly before the War Between the States by William Vest. A few restrained touches of the Greek Revival can still be observed.

(Right) One of the outbuildings of the KERR HOUSE possesses an outer stairway whose pedimented roof has been adapted as a pigeon house.

The 18th Century owner of the KERR HOUSE kept a jewelry shop here and set up a brick kiln nearby. This aroused the indignation of the Burgesses, and Alexander Kerr never got very far in the brick business.

The Old Kitchen of the KERR HOUSE has been transformed into an atmospheric shop for the sale of books, etchings and old prints. Facing it on Blair Street is a row of gnarled paper mulberry trees.

This cheerful little house facing the Raleigh Tavern is known as PURDIE'S DWELLING. It has been known as the home of Alexander Purdie, Public Printer and onetime Publisher of the "Virginia Gazette."

PURDIE'S DWELLING as it appears from the site of the King's Arms Tavern. The original house was purchased by Alexander Purdie in 1767. The present structure is a reconstruction.

The PUBLIC RECORDS OFFICE, a low brick building near the Capitol, was built to store the Colony's records after the Capitol burned in 1747. Popularly known as "The Secretary's Office" it was used as a Chancery Court.

The BLAND-WETHERBURN HOUSE, now privately owned and unrestored, was once the home of Virginia's famed patriot, Richard Bland. Built in the early years of the 18th Century, it was sold to Henry Wetherburn, formerly keeper of the Raleigh Tavern, who later ran this inn under his own name.

An autumnal view of the outbuildings of CHARLTON'S INN. In the foreground is the site of the KING'S ARMS TAVERN, across from the Raleigh Tavern, where one of the new projects of Colonial Williamsburg will take form. This authentic tavern will soon be rebuilt to provide added accommodations for visitors.

A springtime, back-fence view of CHARLTON'S INN and its whitewashed kitchen. George Washington mentions this inn at least seven times in his diaries. The present restored structure contains part of the original inn.

Washington apparently found CHARLTON'S INN more reposeful as an overnight stopping place than the more public Raleigh Tavern, where, however, he often dined. This view shows the outbuildings of the Inn.

The BRICK HOUSE TAVERN, providing "16 Good Rooms for Ladies and Gentlemen," is a comfortable guest house, situated on the Duke of Gloucester Street and operated by the Williamsburg Lodge. This is one of the few Williamsburg buildings of which an existing architectural plan still remains.

13

The charm and comfort of the accommodations in the BRICK HOUSE TAVERN are foreshadowed by this cheerful brick facade. It is raised well above the street and marked by three double doors, each approached by wide steps.

A chain store becomes hardly recognizable when disguised in the Williamsburg manner.

The Shop of the BRICK HOUSE TAVERN has a very distinctive street facade. This is also used as a guest house.

The NANCY CAMP HOUSE has been rebuilt on its old foundations adjoining the Brick House Tavern. The date of the original house is uncertain, but it was bought in 1770 by James Anderson, blacksmith and public armorer. The next year he rented the house to William Drinkard who, providentially named for the purpose, opened it as a tavern. Nancy Anderson, later the wife of George Camp, apparently inherited the house, which was destroyed by fire in 1842.

Through a screen of boxwood hedges, whitewashed picket fences and dogwood blossoms, the camera catches only a fugitive glimpse of the gardens of the NANCY CAMP HOUSE.

A garden path at the NANCY CAMP HOUSE provides strong contrasts in black and white.

The garden kitchen of the NANCY CAMP HOUSE has an exceptionally massive kitchen chimney.

The MARY STITH SHOP offers a study in authentic Colonial brickwork. The modern bricks used to achieve this 18th Century effect, were made in Williamsburg under the supervision of the architects and builders.

Vegetable gardens take on a definite allure with the help of a Colonial background. This garden belongs to the reconstructed ORLANDO JONES HOUSE. Behind the white picket fence is the Mary Stith Shop.

Adjoining the Nancy Camp House, shown here in the background, is the small story-and-a-half MARY STITH SHOP, a livable little structure which boasts one of the rare bay windows on the Duke of Gloucester Street.

In the garden behind the MARY STITH SHOP is this small restored building whose roof has a decided overhang. Once a tinsmith's shop, it was supposedly used for the manufacture of ordnance during the Revolution.

Many a critic would select CAPTAIN ORR'S DWELLING as the most perfect pitch-roofed cottage in Williamsburg.
An informal garden, well packed with boxwood, adjoins the house and provides a restful stop for the pedestrian.

Highlighted with dogwood blossoms, CAPTAIN ORR'S DWELLING looks particularly inviting over the rail fence which borders Colonial Street.

One of the narrowest and most beguiling streets in Williamsburg is Colonial Street. At the point where it crosses the Duke of Gloucester Street are two pitch-roofed houses of great charm. The white cottage is the ORLANDO JONES HOUSE. At the right is a detail of Captain Orr's Dwelling.

Back fence gazers will enjoy themselves thoroughly in the cheerful area behind CAPTAIN ORR'S DWELLING. One secret of the charm of Williamsburg back yards is that they are not marred by the apparition of the Monday morning wash hung out to dry. Clothes lines are provided, but they are low and artfully concealed.

Spring blossoms in the garden of the LIGHTFOOT HOUSE.

A particularly seductive stretch of the Duke of Gloucester Street lies before CAPTAIN ORR'S DWELLING, with the compact white form of the Lightfoot House in the background.

A slender dogwood silhouettes itself against the shadow of the house which Captain Hugh Orr, blacksmith and "Man of Property," mentioned in an advertisement as early as 1739. The shutters and clapboards of the house are painted in contrasting tones of warm grey, set off by white trim.

The LIGHTFOOT HOUSE has had a decided influence upon American domestic architecture. It is something of a curiosity, in that its projecting gambrel roof actually advances the three dormer windows beyond the plane of the first floor facade. The house came into the possession of Philip Lightfoot, wealthy merchant, planter and attorney of Yorktown, by 1747. He served on the Governor's Council and apparently acquired a Williamsburg house as a convenience during "Publick Times."

The "Dutch-roofed" Lightfoot House as it appeared in 1936. In the foreground is an atmospheric doghouse. Dimly in the distance is the old Williamsburg Inn, now departed in favor of Chowning's Tavern.

A springtime glimpse of the outbuildings of the Lightfoot House.

The sidewalk is arched with branches in the reposeful vicinity of the Lightfoot House.

Our path now leads to Francis Street, which parallels the Duke of Gloucester Street on the south. Here is the BARRAUD HOUSE, an ample pitch-roofed structure, the exact date of which is unknown. It was acquired prior to 1796 by the Williamsburg physician, Dr. Philip Barraud.

Before it was restored in 1941 the BARRAUD HOUSE was still a handsome edifice. A graceful porch has been added and the ground floor windows have been shortened somewhat. The old kitchen has also been rebuilt.

A detail of the facade of the restored BARRAUD HOUSE. It is interesting to note that this and most of the other restored buildings in Williamsburg have been roofed with a fireproof shingle which bears a remarkable resemblance to the original wooden shingle of Colonial times.

Williamsburg is replete with unexpected vistas through garden gates. One of these glimpses is found at the EWING HOUSE, where its whitewashed gate and outbuildings form a frame for the distant Powell-Hallam House.

The sedate EWING HOUSE on Francis Street, was once owned by Ebenezer Ewing. Its second story windows do not have pedimented roofs, unlike those of most Williamsburg houses. A forge has been rebuilt in the back yard.

The MOODY HOUSE, a story-and-a-half dwelling of 18th Century tradition, was owned by the Moody family, whose ancestral French name was Modé. It is now used as a guest house for patrons of the Williamsburg Inn.

The courtyard kitchen of the MOODY HOUSE serves as a compact lodge for guests of the Williamsburg Inn. The upper portion of its stocky chimney is free standing.

FRANCIS STREET on a May morning. Under the lacy foliage of a spreading elm this comes to life again as an idyllic village thoroughfare of other days, free of automobiles, signboards, telephone poles and wires.

The POWELL-HALLAM HOUSE, a discreet and charming gambrel-roofed structure on Francis Street, was built shortly after 1753 by Benjamin Powell, a leading carpenter who installed the steeple on Bruton Parish Church and made repairs on the Capitol, Governor's Palace and the Old Gaol. Later it was the home of the noted surgeon, Dr. Thomas Powell.

The POWELL-HALLAM HOUSE was moved here from its original site on York Road in 1930. It is believed that this was once the home of Sarah Hallam, a popular actress and dancing school teacher.

The ORRELL HOUSE, last of a group of four distinguished houses on the south side of Francis Street, closely resembles the Lightfoot house. It was acquired by John Orrell sometime early in the 19th Century.

Detail of the facade of the ORRELL HOUSE.

The sunny front doorway of THE QUARTER.

Every year a certain number of fortunate families make this little whitewashed cottage their headquarters while they are in Williamsburg. It is known as THE QUARTER, and it was inhabited by Negroes during most of the 19th Century. Now it has been restored as a guest house of the Williamsburg Inn, with a scale of comfort in decided contrast to its former primitive state. The magnificent willow in the foreground is now departed, a victim of old age and a high wind.

This wistful photographer has envied the guests of THE QUARTER most, I believe, at that moment in the morning when a tempting hot breakfast is pedalled down to them in an insulated velocipede.

At sunset all objects cast long shadows along Francis Street. Here the camera dodges behind the shadow of a tree trunk and points toward the Market Square for one of this book's rare "atmospheric" views.

A most individual picket fence and a dogwood in bloom lend highlights to this view of the BRACKEN HOUSE, owned by the Reverend John Bracken, an eminent and sometimes controversial citizen of Williamsburg.

Rear view of the BRACKEN HOUSE. Its owner was a longtime Rector of Bruton Parish Church (1773-1818), a member of the College faculty, Mayor of Williamsburg, and for a time, a Bishop of Virginia and President of the College of William and Mary.

The architectural grace of the BRACKEN HOUSE is somewhat overshadowed in this picture by the contortions of two aged paper mulberry trees.

The full impressive height of the East Chimney of the BRACKEN HOUSE is shown here.

Williamsburg kitchen doors have a character of their own. This one belongs to the ORLANDO JONES HOUSE.

To the exacting traveler, Williamsburg offers a richly appointed hostelry with the highest standards of comfort, cuisine and service—the WILLIAMSBURG INN. Designed by the firm of Perry, Shaw and Hepburn, it was opened in April, 1937. During World War II its facilities were reserved for Army and Navy officers and their families.

The south facade of the WILLIAMSBURG INN reveals an architectural style which was popular at the Springs of Virginia in the early 19th Century. The decorations and furnishings of the Inn are from the Regency period.

The south terrace of the WILLIAMSBURG INN has some of the atmosphere of a Continental spa. From this comfortable spot, guests look out upon the Inn's own golf course. An outdoor swimming pool is a short distance away.

Besides serving as a central information center, the CRAFT HOUSE contains an exhibit of authentic copies of Williamsburg furniture and furnishings which are available to the public. The Craft Program has made possible the manufacture of actual replicas of Colonial pieces, all fashioned with the skill and thoroughness of the early craftsmen. Among the articles reproduced are furniture, silverware, mirrors, pewter, glassware, china, silks, printed fabrics, paints, needlework, wall papers, wrought iron, brasswork, writing accessories, books and prints.

The ALLEN-BYRD HOUSE, "a good brick dwelling with four rooms on each floor," was built prior to 1770, perhaps in the early part of the 18th Century, by William Allen, who later sold it to William Byrd III. Its Francis Street facade is cut up into five bays, and its garden fence is one of the most elaborate in Williamsburg.

The rear of the ALLEN-BYRD HOUSE is severe behind its paled back fence. This facade contains only three bays. The original brickwork with glazed headers is well preserved and still shows signs of 19th Century appendages, since removed.

The Kitchen and outbuildings of the ALLEN-BYRD HOUSE are extensive. They are sheathed in wide weatherboards, painted a rich maroon color, and set off with white trim. An unusual basket weave fence appears here.

The WILLIAMSBURG LODGE, a commodious, well planned structure built in 1939, has since earned the esteem of an ever increasing list of patrons who appreciate its hospitality, comfort, good cooking and reasonable prices.

Dogwood days are few in Williamsburg, but when they arrive they transform this empty lot facing the Market Square into a flowery bower. At the left is the Powder Magazine and beyond is the Randolph-Peachy House.

The PUBLIC MAGAZINE, long called "The Powder Horn," was erected for reasons of safety in an open area on the southern half of the Market Square. Completed in 1716, it was used to hold military stores and explosives from then until 1775. Its brick walls were two feet thick but in 1755, during the apprehension caused by the French and Indian Wars, encircling walls ten feet high were added. Early in the morning of April 20, 1775, Governor Dunmore, alarmed by signs of revolt, had the powder removed from this magazine to avoid its seizure by the populace. This ill-considered act contributed to the surging discontent which led to the outbreak of Revolution in Virginia. After these epic days, the building was used as a Market House, dancing school, Baptist meeting house and finally as a livery stable. A guard of twelve men was kept over the magazine from 1756 to 1762. The guardhouse where they lived is to be rebuilt on the Market Square.

(Left) Detail inside the enclosure of the PUBLIC MAGAZINE.

The MARKET SQUARE is serene in this picture, in contrast to the turbulence which marked the scene during Colonial times. Town Fairs which attracted all the countryside were held here in April and December.

The PUBLIC MAGAZINE and its octagonal wall were rescued from an uncertain fate by the Association for the Preservation of Virginia Antiquities in 1889. It is owned by this Society, and was restored by Colonial Williamsburg in 1935.

The MARKET SQUARE TAVERN, a Williamsburg institution of much significance in Colonial days, has been restored on its old site and now serves as a commodious guest house for patrons of the Williamsburg Lodge. One of its restored public rooms, shown above, now serves as a lounge. The original Tavern was probably built in 1749 on a lot leased to John Dixon. By 1771 it was owned by Gabriel Maupin, saddler and harness-maker, and later by Peter Rob DeNeufville, another French-American. Other proprietors included a tailor, a merchant, and a barber and wigmaker.

(Left) Detail of the facade of the MARKET SQUARE TAVERN.

The hospitable, vine-covered facade of the MARKET SQUARE TAVERN faces the Duke of Gloucester Street and adjoins what once was a very active trading center. Large markets were held here at regular intervals in the 18th Century. Hucksters and farmers shouted hoarsely and sold produce directly from their wagons. At the semi-annual fairs, prizes were given to farmers bringing in the best draft horses for sale, and to those bringing the most cows, sheep, steers and hogs.

Innkeepers displayed keen insight in selecting their locations in those days, choosing either to be close to the Capitol or bordering the Market Square. At least fifteen taverns competed for the business of the Burgesses and lesser officials near the Capitol, while the MARKET SQUARE TAVERN and its neighbors catered more to the farmer trade.

The white frame kitchen of the MARKET SQUARE TAVERN has been rebuilt with the usual immense chimney. It faces an informal garden, one of several whose flowered paths and restful benches are open to the public.

Whitewashed outbuildings, stables and paddocks are grouped around the garden of the MARKET SQUARE TAVERN, in the 18th Century manner.

The whitewashed well cover in the garden of the MARKET SQUARE TAVERN glistens with reflected light on a summer afternoon.

Another individual well cover adjoins the newly built James City Courthouse.

A picket fence only makes the gardens of the MARKET SQUARE TAVERN more inviting.

Our path leads across the Market Square to the REPITON HOUSE, an unconventional four-chimney dwelling. It was owned by John Greenhow, the Williamsburg merchant who sold gentlemen's boots and a wide variety of merchandise at prices so high that they aroused heated protests among the populace. The house was acquired by Joseph Repiton in 1810. Recently it has been rebuilt, together with a dairy, well and kitchen. Adjoining it is a modest little brick building whose walls remain unchanged since Colonial days. It is the old "Debtor's Prison" (left) so called by local tradition.

The Repiton House and its small neighbor, THE BOOT & SHOEMAKER'S SHOP, form a compact group on the edge of the Market Square. In normal times a bootmaker is at work in this shop, making costume shoes for Colonial Williamsburg. Along with several of the other Craft Shops, it was closed during the war years.

(Right) Detail of the facade of the REPITON HOUSE, typical of the more modest Colonial street fronts.

The sign which hangs in front of the TRAVIS HOUSE informs the hungry wayfarer of the "Good Eating" which awaits him within. Countless guests of recent years could assure the wayfarer that he will not be disappointed

From a gastronomic point of view, this is by far the most satisfying segment of the Duke of Gloucester Street, for here gather the epicures, the gourmets and the informed critics of fine Virginia cooking. The TRAVIS HOUSE offers its guests charming hospitality, a selection of notable Southern dishes and skillful service. They dine by candlelight in the evening, and an inviting table in the holly garden awaits them at mid-day.

The TRAVIS HOUSE, originally built about 1765, was moved by Colonial Williamsburg to its present location from its old site on South Henry Street. It rests on the foundations of a house once owned by John Greenhow.

The narrow brick gable end and the shallow dormers of the TRAVIS HOUSE are far from usual.

During the warm months, guests of the TRAVIS HOUSE can enjoy Southern cooking in garden pavilions.

The JOHN CUSTIS TENEMENT, also known as the Maupin-Dixon House, occupies a choice site facing Bruton Parish Church and the Palace Green. The original house, of which this is a replica, served as a multiple dwelling. While sheltering Continental troops in 1776 it was destroyed by fire.

Another back yard approach enables the camera to catch an informal view of the JOHN CUSTIS TENEMENT and its outbuildings.

This small framed house was the home of JAMES GALT, the first keeper of the nearby Asylum for "lunatics, idiots and other persons of unsound mind." When the asylum was ravaged by fire in 1885, this cottage was spared.

When the restoration of Williamsburg was undertaken, the JAMES GALT HOUSE was moved to its present site facing Bruton Parish Church. Over the picket fence one gets an unexpected glimpse of the church tower.

One of Williamsburg's most beloved gardens lies between the CUSTIS TENE-MENT and the half-hidden James Galt House. It is a formal squared garden with brick paths and triangular beds surrounded by low box hedges. Luxuriant hedges of untrimmed box frame the enclosure, which glistens with old fashioned flowers from April to October.

(Left) The COLE SHOP, a Colonial store, was probably built by Charles Taliaferro, who owned the house to the west of it. It consisted originally of a single room. Later a lean-to was added to the west side, and an overhanging roof was built to shelter a well. Today it still serves as a book and print shop, and is well known to Williamsburg visitors.

The outbuildings of the TALIAFERRO-COLE HOUSE stretch out along Nassau Street, the last side street which our path crosses before returning to the business community. The original house was the home of Charles Taliaferro, well known maker of coaches and riding chairs. He sold it to Jesse Cole in 1804.

The formal gardens and picturesque outbuildings of the BRYAN HOUSE are comparatively new additions to the Williamsburg scene, as this dwelling was one of the last to be reconstructed.

The last stop on our tour of old Williamsburg is at the BRYAN HOUSE. Its colorful and luxuriant flower beds leave the visitor with a thoroughly pleasant parting impression as this pictorial promenade comes to its conclusion.

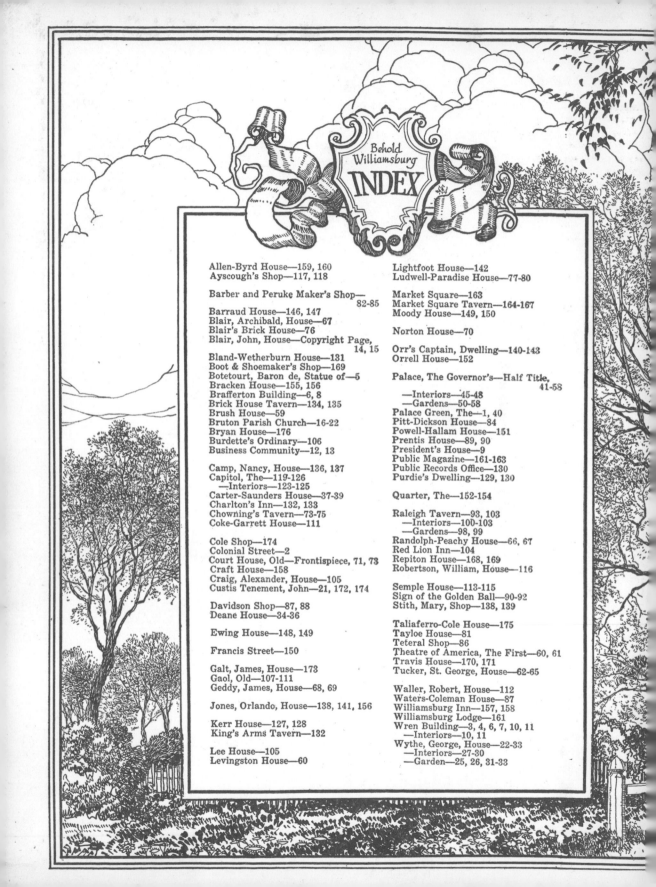

Behold
Williamsburg
INDEX